Red F

SASHA DUGDALE was born in Suss[...]
worked for the British Council i[...]
Russian New Writing Project with the Royal Court Theatre. She
currently works as a translator and consultant for the Royal Court
and other theatre companies. Many of her translations have been
staged, one of which, *Plasticine* by Vassily Sigarev, won the *Evening
Standard* Award for Most Promising Playwright. She has published
two collections of translations of Russian poetry and, with Carcanet,
two collections of her own poetry, *Notebook* (2003) and *The Estate*
(2007). In 2003 she received an Eric Gregory Award.

Also by Sasha Dugdale from Carcanet / OxfordPoets

Notebook
The Estate

SASHA DUGDALE

Red House

Oxford*Poets*

CARCANET

Acknowledgements

Earlier versions of some of the poems in this collection were published in *Agenda*, *The Irish Times*, *Poetry London*, *Poetry Magazine*, *Poetry Review*, *Idenity Parade* (Bloodaxe, 2010) and *Best British Poetry 2011* (Salt, 2011).

First published in Great Britain in 2011 by
Carcanet Press Limited
Alliance House
Cross Street
Manchester M2 7AQ

A CIP catalogue record for this book is available from the British Library

ISBN 978 1 906188 02 3

The publisher acknowledges financial assistance from Arts Council England

Typeset by XL Publishing Services, Tiverton
Printed and bound in England by SRP Ltd, Exeter

To Max and Harriet

Contents

Maldon

And there on the coast like a Chinese lantern hung the sun.
Whatever you do, you should not let them pour off the half-island
To mix with the birds and the silts, said the wise woman.
For there they will become us – body of our body
Blood of our blood. And theirs and our flesh will hang
On bushes, like the undershirt of Midas. Dead throats
Will shirk in the sedge like spiderwebs, whispering
Of how the victors took pliers to teeth and chopped charms out.
No one left to remember the women, but they were deer
Fleet and hunted, springing sideways, stunned by a fist.
And when the sun rises, it will seem to our ancestors that a new race
Has come up out of the sea, dripping with gold, crueller than the last.

Red House

The red house lies without the parish of the soul.
The frozen trees, the swings in the grey yard, the slow sweeping fans
Of brushes in light snow, and how that bus stops every day
Just beyond the red house and picks up.
Stay or leave? There is no addressing the Lord
For we are plain beyond that, but isn't that white round a hole
In the sky where he once sat? Many of the shadows
Look up in their sickness, point with their aimless guns
And spout aimless rounds, and now one may hit
And one piece of bright shot will slip into that winter sun
And tear it, so that tomorrow it limps and spits sunset
All bleeding day. Red house, red house, forgive us such trespasses
For aren't we the twice blessed, having lived through stranger
                                                            weather

And having known you, red house?

★

Starlings in the loft and eaves of the red house
And the nestlings peep and pip at intervals, heard in rooms throughout
By the day-sick and the unfit for work. There was a golden age
For sure: there is always a golden age, like a shower of gold
Sweeter at a distance, perpendicular to the beloved body
Siring leaden times and leaden rivers. Now the madman,
Calling out of his window, denounces his long-dead neighbours,
The starlings pass him off, stuttering, the starlings passing through –
How birdcalls make sense of sorrow and suffering
Which is subject to hyper-inflation and loses its own mortal currency
In numbers. Red house, I see you in the city, on the plain
By the roadside and the railway. You are never in the mountains
Or by the sea. The smell of you is homely and nauseating
Like the smell of all humankind.

★

There was a woman who left the red house with her baby.
Her own mother waved from the window, a taxi took them away,
Daughter and granddaughter and then they were gone.
The woman dreamt at night of the red house:
The gaping letterboxes; the stink of tobacco and piss
Which fits so snugly, like a baby's bonnet;
Her own footsteps climbing the stairwell ahead of her;
The tender annoyance of a wasp trapped on a landing.
Her mother stood with dumbbells in the kitchen
Swinging her hips this way and that, swinging her eyes
This way and that, wishing they were real bells she held
To clash and peal about her in a passion:
For never in all her great maternal struggling
Had she once considered such a silence.

★

Once a man brought home a bear to the red house.
A zoo-bear, still a cub, and muzzled and harnessed.
The children were kept inside as it played. The man smoked
And twitched the reins, and ground cigarettes under his heel.
The bear snuffled under the bench and grubbed up shit and
sweetwrappers.
The bear's sojourn was a gift of sorts, for the man was a romantic
And hoped his girl would relent when she saw the creature
And bring them milk in a saucer and titbits, and humanwarmth.
Until she let him in he would sleep on the landing with the bear
And teach him to dance on his hind legs, up the steps and down
In an endless manbeast cha-cha, paws clattering, feet slapping
His humming summoning succour from the stairwell.
The bear they took on the third day; it went well enough back
into the light.
The man threw himself from the window, and he was lamed for life.

★

All the world is beyond the padded door of the flat.
A man once followed a girl into the red house and caught her on
                                                                the stairs.

He held a black knife in his fist, and motioned.
Others are ready for this relationship, but not her:
She reflects at length upon the imposed hostilities
She anticipates the knife pressing down on her pink skin
Until it gives, she suspects they might never be friends
Her and him, and all the while she begs and screams and whispers
Please, playing the part assigned to her with a blade's gesture.
The wrought iron design of the banisters catches her eye –
It would be designed by a man, that, in its hard superfluous beauty
And knocked into place by another man, and then forgotten
Until now, until she stood and wondered: why vines and sickles
                                                                and sheaves?
Little girl, he says, I have done with this. Go now. Go. Please.

★

Imagine this: there is a room in the red house,
Infernal clutter, brocades and periodicals, and a mirror full of gloaming
And when the place is empty, she takes a basin of apples
Into this room and sits on the bed. There she is, in the mirror.
The room is not fresh. Everything here was bought in another time
By the long-spent, oft-bereaved who own fruit knives
And sugar tongs and no memory of the provenance of anything –
Except the hard little apples, which fall so close to the tree.
So she escapes from childhood and taking refuge
In the red house inhales the historical sweat
The ancient hair-grease of its inhabitants
Who have sloughed off desperate times
And left their wearied skins
Folded breast-up like nightshirts on the pillow.

★

I could be happy and gainful without the red house
But it draws me to its mineral seam like home
When I am without the red house, I am without
And when I am within, I am undone.
A fist, a bomb will not destroy it
A hurtful letter, or a threat:
It is made of wasp-thought and saliva
But holds its own like footwear made of lead.
I cannot find it, should I want to
I have mislaid it now for several hundred years
It drags me in, fisherhouse of peoples
It spins me out, it shows me empty rooms.
The Red House lies within, I have heard it beating
The Red House lies without the parish of the soul.

Perhaps Akhmatova was right
When she wrote who knows what shit
What tip, what pile of waste
Brings forth the tender verse
Like hogweed, like the fat hen under the fence
Like the unbearable present tense
Who knows what ill, what strife
What crude shack of a life
And how it twists sweetly about the broken sill:
Pressingness, another word for honeysuckle
But housewives? Has poetry
Ever deepened in the pail
Was it ever found in the sink, under the table
Did it rise in the oven, quietly able
To outhowl the Hoover?
Does it press more than the children's supper
The sudden sleepless wail?
Did it ever?
It lives. It takes seed
Like the most unforgiving weed
Grows wilder as the child grows older
And spits on dreams, did I say
How it thrives in the ashen family nest
Or how iambs are measured best
Where it hurts:
With the heel of an iron
On the reluctant breast
Of a shirt?

Ten Moons

And then came the ten moons
Full in the sun's glare, and the seraphim,
And it was light all night in the orchards
And on the plains and even in the towns
And mankind rejoiced, because it was now the case
That the wrecking and equivocating could carry on
The pale night long. Mankind rejoiced
And went forth to those places twelve hours of light
Had not made it worth the while to despoil
And gambolled collectively on the cliff tops
And regarded the night-broiling of the sea
Hitherto forbidden, but now opened in festival.
Half the world's time unpeeled and exposed
So fruit might ripen faster and tree flourish higher
And forced photosynthesis green all the land.
Then night ramblers, night-sun-worshippers,
Night-motorists fanned out and made the most
Of spectral light, which bleached out stars and even
The cosy old moon herself, who had
Once held a sickle broadside to the sun, and now
Was a hollow daytime shadow.
Only a few old-believers slept
Hand in hand, shoulder to breast,
As if their lives depended on it, knowing yet
That the morning would bring nothing
Because the day knew no beginning
And had no end.

The Poetry of Earth

The poetry of earth is mostly suppressed
It has been a good while since the cricket rasped
His tickly song from the grate, and the grasshopper
Minded his old green business in the field.
I could no more sing than cling to grass
But all the words I need are notes
There are instruments designed to catch
The water in spate, the ramming wave
The trickle of a jug-throat, but I am dumb
There are tones like cups to fit the measures of elation
But I saw the green from the road and I had none
I know what it means: *my heart for joy did burst!*
To make a path, to live in silent trepidation
Between song and substance
                                        This is a curse.

Michael Blann

There was a hush, then Michael Blann
Stepped out onto the stage. Michael
Blann, with his pipe and his jukebox head
Oh, he's your man.

He has a song for all weathers, a pipe
And a voice and he sings and he roams
He sings to the wind and a dog of how
The trees are all bare and Jack's come home.

He's a thin voice, like a spider thread
On days when the sun is late and fine
Live and let live, sings Michael Blann
The wind yields not, but the hills is mine.

He's no call for fate passing over
His sheep are all angels, the stars are his lords
He'll play any part the clouds should fancy
To humble tunes and hand-me-down words

The acts are written in briar strands
And the Pharisees are leaves in the air
I likes a drop pipes Michael Blann
Sing follow hark forward the innocent hare.

He wore to his end a clutch of sheep's wool
To show the gods that Michael Blann
Went alone, alone for most of his years
But crossed the hills a singing man.

A Ballad without Rhyme

This is a ballad without rhyme.
This is a ballad without sound of any sort.
In time they found the subject of this tune
And she was much more than the sum of her parts.

And how did it happen? That with her thick brown paws
And face lined all over like an exercise book
She would be carried the night athwart
On a star, trailing a winding sheet.

But I saw her in the kitchen. She was twiddling the tablecloth
Not praying, but talking to her late child
Admonishing his invisible boyhood
For the mess of leaden soldiers in the yard

The three days unmade bed. Banging the lid
Of the salt-caddy. Fine loneliness
For the house, half-broken, stood
In a mouth of trees and upon a waste

And where the bench in the yard
Had worn the imprint of an arse
Half a century in the making
There now was a bare place

And what she had was thyme
Stolen from the hillside,
Scenting every cupboard, room
Wild thyme for embalming.

So all the armies are passed –
She kept keys in a casserole
With cuttings, letters and a crust
A needle and an awl.

So solitary her movement I nearly cried out
How I need this rhyme! This coming of age
When all ages are equally mine
And only gibbets and gristle to illuminate.

Make history of us, good calm history
In tapestries and ballad form
I desire a painting of her, in the bed's dent
A relic, a stain in the shroud, a rent

Instead I have the barren machinery:
The grease, the rags and the sod.
Skimmed of all her martyrdom she stands
Wrathful, impossible to behold.

Dawn Chorus

29 March 2010

Every morning since the time changed
I have woken to the dawn chorus
And even before it sounded, I dreamed of it
Loud, unbelievably loud, shameless, raucous

And once I rose and twitched the curtains apart
Expecting the birds to be pressing in fright
Against the pane like passengers
But the garden was empty and it was night

Not a slither of light at the horizon
Still the birds were bawling through the mists
Terrible, invisible
A million small evangelists

How they sing: as if each had pecked up a smouldering coal
Their throats singed and swollen with song
In dissonance as befits the dark world
Where only travellers and the sleepless belong

Fish's Dream

I thought I would dive into the pool like them
But found myself skimming the surface like a pond-skater
The water was the dead spit of the sky
I saw my children kissing strangers
My son was mouthing a girl, the devotion
Of two fighting fish, he wants me far
From the river of his life, back to swimming the ocean
With the fleeting ghosts of kelt
That pay visit only when it is the season.
And so I am spawned and held
In the sea's own shuttle
To be a glistening return
Containing my own river-reason
And muscle-mettle
Washed into unknown elation
Caught in the strange current
Of homing, homing!
The womb abhorrent
The body teeming
The water – from here –
A silvery migration.

Lifting the bedcovers and there
The scent of little bodies, their secretions
Their feet, bellies, mouths and hair
Animals overwintering for the season
Of a single night, and how the air
Surges into, under, like water through the horses
Of Augeas, cold on the sweet, fetid, bare
Skins, and that smell is fled contorted
With a small grimace out to the spare
Grey morning, all I embrace
Evaporating in the cool earth's care
Less animal now the opening faces
Their clothes lie folded on the chair
Not yet awake, nor soon aware.

Out of Town

Out in the open fields go the good ghosts
The ones who released from heaven leap and croon
Who were locked to the old church beneath the bypass
Until their heartstones were piled to make more room
They come and go now like vapours through the grates
They come and go, released from mortal flesh and weight

And parade through the unsown fields of wild oats
And meadows of agrimony and clover
And reach a hill, the wedge end of a fell,
And this too the revelling ghosts fly over
All the better to reach the fingers of the town
The town's sightless fingers groping for their own.

Ghosts like to find the middle point
The place where open country runs to ground
Amongst the out-of-town superstores
Allotments, cemeteries, stolen vehicle pounds
Where roads peter into ruts of ancient use
And owners turn unwanted house pets loose.

The blossoming of the end, the frayed flex of the beginning:
The pilgrim enters in, passes through and out.
The ghosts however go no further
The place of worship for the immaterial devout
Might be fixed here, by a vague averaging of town and field
On a site leasehold under offer / current yield

Or down a twitten, where the sad ghosts of weeds
Proliferate all the summer long
Where the walls are sprayed with piss and broken bottles
But morning is coated in silver light and song
And the snakehead streetlamps warm a gap
In the hoary canopies of each year's cold snap

This is where the town fucks sincerely
Exhibits its most human shape
The ones who are destitute or nearly
The ones without an honest place to sleep
Come here and in the morning when the birds sing like crazy
They walk a few yards into the wet green and weep

But ghosts are beyond all human weakness
They throng to service stations as to holy wells
That wherever the world tips upon its axis
They won't be nearer or further then from hell
The listless ghosts, unfreighted, aimless, flit
And need a wasteland to level their spirit.

I have met people who spend their nervous youth
In cities, fearing even the weather that blew
From empty places, beaches, heaths
And others, who gorged on wide skies, those too
When the time came, lifted up their souls and died
And in the hereafter craved the lonely divide

I know a few of us to whom the place is already sweet
Its copses of rusting cars, its pointless verge
The ache it puts in place of a deep heart
As this life and the one beyond converge
Here the poisoned Lethe trickles under weeds
That scatter, year after year, their unloved seeds.

No nearer to heaven here, or hell
No talk of salvation here, or ruination
All that can be done of both is done
The mind has made of both a desolation
And in this desolation at last a space
Where no-man's-land might be an honest place.

A lorry driver sleeping in his cab
Two walkers wearing hats and carrying shells
The ghosts are in each blade of grass
Each blade of grass a heaven and a hell
The pilgrims come amongst them and pass through
And one looked much like me and one like you.

Amazing Grace

It was sweet, but so short
You're not being honest, he said
And I was filled
But bent under the weight

Some bodily discomfort helps
I was lost, I'd know
Not honest, like that, repeating
The words, but I see now.

Grace, which precious, like to mercy
Falls, dissolves like snow
I wish something were forever
I was lost, I should know.

The shadows fret me, if I'm honest
Woman, you can fucking shut your
And all that folding and unfolding linen
Heart, be honest, hold your

Weeds grow often and are undaunted
By fingers scrabbling in the dirt
Amazing – graceless now, but living –
How the hell to fill a wretch like her.

Plainer Sailing (Alzheimer's)

for A.W.

She walked then: pale and unbent
Frail as a cloud, filled with a cloud's watered light
And all the ropes were gone, and the language unlearnt
And vital knots of past and future long untied.

There was once no sailing without the augur on board,
Who shaped each day and told what tumbled past,
Who sought the truth in feathered gore
Whilst others watched from the crow's nest.

She too surveyed the calm, and was concerned:
What to make of all the signs, for the sea is rarely blank.
And there was a circling, a moment returned
When daughter was mother, and there the sun shrunk

And bent and was narrow at the line of sky
And still the clouds twisted and birds flew
All above at that time there was no end to life
And no end to other brightnesses at least as true

That seem like mirages now. For signs were massing
To display themselves in a common light:
They did all surely point to the one passing
Of pale day into paler night.

I can only be who I am
Said the storm as it drew its crow wings about the tree
The tree knew that smell
It flinched and held itself small and rigid
If it had gods it would ask them for mercy
Splintering its thousand green flags
In the storm's great embrace
But the tree knows loneliness too
Learnt from the caterpillar and the bird
And godlessness, which is next to survival
And a hundred other small skills
Which are barely noticeable from the sky
But have counted for something grand
In the hill's meadow-grass.
Remember we walked its grey trunk
Over the fluent stream
It gave us passage, but no word of what lay beyond

Moor

And for days it seemed she was climbing
Knees bloodied – as quick as she knew how
So that one said to another: hey Phil
Did you see how fast that girl was walking?
But as she herself could see nothing, she could not tell
It was just an endless effort of heather and fern
As rancid as closed windows and pencil shavings
And the red water tippling from flush to ocean
So slowly fast her walking was but nothing
To its coronation dance. She had heard of men
Who married this place with its hares
And laid their heads on stones and begot
With water making utterance of its sifting
And shifting and spouting –
And after that chasing quivering throatful
All the women in the world were no more than
Spoons of cough medicine.
How well she knew her limits
Although she had jumped the golden trickling
Just like a boy, was as stupid as any man.
When he comes, she said, and takes the water
Over me, then what shall I be?
Faster and faster she goes, plaiting the fibres of grasses
Hoping the sky will take pity on her
Make a rapid stream of me that he might love me deeper
Put finger and thumb in me, and nape of neck
And break the lip of me with startled face
And we will be quite apart, and yet
Down in that city, shivering and shining with rain
He will long for the red halo, climbing his forehead
Clinging in drops to his shoulder, lifted in his hands
For certain downfall.

Prince's

24 January 2011

Yesterday afternoon, one of the shortest of the year
When the hills were dark with a night not yet come
And the high street silent and all the doors closed
I learnt that Prince's would soon be gone.

A haberdasher's is hardly a terrible loss
It was not a place I ever went in much
Although I admired the near-redundant, near-extinct
Art of dressing the provincial shopfront

The quaint pre-war touches: how the ladies' shirts
Were tied in pretty ribbons at their waists
And jaunty trilbies floated over dancing jackets
Bearing pockets of silken hanky points.

And often I have seen gentlemen cradling paper bags
Of slippers and shoes with new black heels
Slipping out from under the shop's sun blind
And disappearing down the modern street

Thirty years now. I walked to school that way
Saw the seasons come and go in their displays:
Nightshirts hanging from green hoops in spring
Snowmen holding Christmas stockings in branched fingers

You would call it an ordinary shop on an ordinary street
And not somewhere the dream's particles might lie.
The lady serving me lost her husband last year
She's glad it's over, she says, she needs more time.

I have not the wit to offer any comfort
The window unadorned reads 'closing – end of line'.
How the fact of it can suddenly strike you
Yes, time is good, I say. I'm sure things heal with time.

But time flows down the high street like a river
Like the Spital, which exceeds its muddy confines
Each winter, and the rest of the long year
Whispers insistent at the back of the shopper's mind.

I should be able to escape this honest town
There must be places where creation sings aloud
Can you not hear it? How its blasting trumpet-wind
Blows the streams back up to higher ground.

This next spring we will wade up the Spital river
And shrug the town from us, and leave it lie
How the stream narrows now and lightens
Its pulse grows feeble, its breath a tiny sigh –

In the window I see the yards of draper's tape,
Which once knew the height of a body, its mortal breadth.
So night falls once again with the roaring of a river
Indifferent to its very depths.

Doggy Life

After Auden's Musée des Beaux-Arts

I have my doggy life to consider
Others may do the falling from the sky
I make a home in the ripe corn
And count birds and insects yappily.

It is the very health of me
That matters – gleaming coat and fangs
And mind untroubled by psychosis
Beyond the usual things –

Yesterday, for instance, a magpie,
Several old and chewy balls
And a nameless mess I worry
Until my impatient owner yells.

The endless doggy acquisition:
Bones and feathers, piss and spit
The innocent horse's whisking tail,
The innocent horse's tumbling shit.

A dog like me lives by a camp
A dog like me licks hangman's hands
That taste of sweat and hempen rope
And nicotine and scented soap.

On Beauty

Those children with their yellow-painted faces and tangled wreaths
Of green and berry and stick, they have waited
A thousand years to be born again, and here they are
Gracious and grateful, and still with impacted movement.
I call their legs shanks, because they are as slender as forearms
Their flesh is at one with their bone; their hair with their flesh
I ascribe to them no existential complaints, no nervous diseases
Constipation, chewed nails, hard skin, tooth decay, bad breath
Their soul is as large as their body, precisely,
Their body fit to glove such a splendid invisible organ.
I have cracked my glasses on a stone and I have a blister.
Lord, give me strength to protect these children
From the soldiers, ex-soldiers, arse-fuckers, shitmongers
The unclean, unwashed, the simple, the hopeless, the West
With its bulbous self-determination, all those people who kiss
Death and say: I don't know I don't know all the while
From ice-creams, cheap sweets and tin signs that say: drink cola
And internecine wars and minefields, chemical spills, slicks
Shit, better to die than to live like that. Better to wander Lethe
In shadow, than paint yourself and gambol under the flawed sun.

Asylum

You say the old masters never got it wrong,
But when Goya painted the death of the imagination
It was a lost dog against a usurious yellow sky
And the dog, a hapless creature who had drawn itself
Ten miles on two legs, stared in amazement
To see the man who once fed him from his plate
Reduced to this.

So I felt this week, the vile soil and everything upon it —
The beggar guest kicked from the table
Before his own dog, and even the honest unpicking
Of art performed nightly and in seclusion.
Like any Penelope my armour is resignation
Although I thought I would lift the bow myself
And draw.

By the morning he is gone
And what to make of this?
The prostitutes hang from a beam like mice
The suitors are piled unburied in the yard.
And some say that it is now much better
And others, that it is worse.
So order was restored
I stared in amazement

Song of the Seagull

Ukrainian folksong

Woe, woe, woe to the seagull
Seagull, O poor unhappy bird
She who wove her nest, laid her eggs
By the well-trod road.

Where some young travelling merchants
Stopped to rest and graze their oxen
And chased the gull away,
Stole her little children.

The seagull rose and there she circled,
Then down to the road she hurtled
To the damp, cold earth she falls,
To the men she calls.

'O most kind and noble merchants,
Still so young, no more than children
Give back my little chickens,
My own little children.'

'No, you shall not ever see them,
Nor fold them close, no, I'll not yield
For you'll gather them about you
And fly off to the field.'

'I will never fly away,
I'll stay here, oh I will stay
Here to watch over your oxen,
To mind my little children.'

'Fly, unhappy seagull, fly
To the far green hills, fly
For your children's necks are broken
And in my pot they lie.'

'My children's slim necks are broken,
Dead in your pot they lie,
Then may your oxen sicken
Sicken all and die.

'May you know no journey's end
May your travels last forever
For my children are dead,
Lost to me forever.'

Shepherds

Late June the ghosts of shepherds meet on the hills
And one has his crook with its musket barrel hook
One carries a Bible, and all wear the smock
And listen out for the little bells and the canister bells
Worn by the sheep and the big cattle, carried by the wind
Which shapes the hawthorn into mermaid's hair and open book.

There are those who died on the hills, and those who died in their
                                                            beds,
The haloed, who wear a flame about them, were
Asleep in their wagons, the stove door ajar
The oil lamp tipped. And scores stamp
A last ghastly dawn patrol – their crook a rifle
Cigarettes for their bible.

The hills are not high. High enough
To exist outside us, our low troubles
At the school gates the children look up
And see with a shock of memory
That the earth gathers itself
Into another world
One closer to the sky

Once peopled by shepherds,
Who inherited the high roads from kings and saints
As they passed, withy ropes about their shoulders.
Who spoke little, and wore tall hats
Bawled gently at their dogs,
Who were themselves
Creatures apart

Times when the mist comes up
And rolls like weighted grey
Down the scarp, up there
The cars see their lamps reflected back
A metre ahead, and the back of her is silent
But never like a moor, never fierce like that

She'd carry you back to your own gate
On the palm of her hand – not bury you alive.

Her spine is a landshed, and a land of itself
A land of haunches and shoulders, and glistening fields
Impossible that they weren't in love with her
The kindness of her miles, the smalls of her back,
The blazing white of her summers.

The Bible is her book: she wrote it for her shepherds
To train them in oblivion and seasons
And the time she knows, the slowest time on earth.
She wrote it in chalk, in rabbit droppings, and lady's smock
She wrote it in sweet marjoram and she adorned it with bells
And it has no meaning for anyone, except the shepherds
Who are gone.

All Souls'

After Charles Causley

Summer is over. Autumn's lovely cells
Are collapsing and the yellow pears are underfoot
Call it mellow call it rotten, until the frost comes
And stops the rot like a knife, and the wasps fall midflight
Masses of apples slowly becoming the soil. I am not afraid of the cold
But every year wheels round and its deafening crescendo cut short
When the temperature drops, plummeting like the weighted line
Into the black sea. November, black sea, more terrible than the last –
And only her busy fingers to weave charms, and her laugh
Tickling ribs on All Souls', food and drink enough
For all the dead, when she sees the first frost edging the last leaves.
Oh she proves that life, short life, is the only prize
And don't the dead know it, lifted from the oceans
The cold earth, they nudge the windows and whisper:
Never... ever... been... away...

Annunciation

i.m. Irena Sendler

Take my child, take it quickly now and have
Done by it, do by it as you would any child
And place it in your toolbox, gently
Amongst the pliers and the rags
Anoint it with linseed and make it a bed of copper.

From here in there are two worlds. One bought of this
Transaction, weighed and found wanting,
The other in which the womb is soldered shut daily
Death is your mother, slipping you mercury in her breast milk
Letting the gold from her finger drown in the toilet bowl
Wrenching you from her heart with an iron bar

Take my child, let me never see it again
Let me never feed it again, or run my finger down its spine
Or open its palm and press it against my lead-filled mouth

From here in there are two worlds. One drops like the cold rain
In the cold streets, as you hurry away with your weight of flesh
The other crumples and is gone

*Irena Sendler rescued many children from the Warsaw Ghetto. She entered the Ghetto
on the pretence of inspecting sanitation. Most of the children she saved were orphaned by
the Holocaust.*

The Alphabet of Emigration

Aaron was the first letter of the alphabet
And how it seemed then, a sort of greed
Hugging a name which opened the alphabet not once
But twice, and going on to envelop anteater and antelope
And all manner of beasts, down to the zebra who cantered
To that town, because he had heard the fame of Aaron who took
                                                    everyone.
Alef-bet, from *a* to *zet*, their last possession sold, their books, their gods
Their neighbours, the old kings, the hard winters, gone, gone, gone
And even the memories reduced and wrung out on balconies
Jettisoned like old clothes, shorn like the wolf's fur, the leopard's spots
Ot a do ya the new is much like the old, it has the same horrors
Similar joys, it is only new, Aaron, the first time you hear it
The old creatures brought their mocking tongues, *Aby*
They say to the bears, the cheetahs, their daughters,
If only your souls will be at home, for we look back at the waters
From the bows of a boat, paying out the past
Like a rope which will jam fast, in this, Aaron's place,
Aaron's bath where the carp dive, the eel flitters
Ghosts, says Aaron, like the horses drinking at inlets, the jetties
The cool water, the nightingales, the open river
Stacks inhabited by the lonely stork,
Tracks up to villages, walnut and willow
Empty windows where bills once yellowed
Odessa, Hamburg, Liverpool, Cork
From anywhere in Europe via Rotterdam
Sail on the Zaandijk, the Zyldijk, the Zaandam

Agora

Athens, 2010

All along the road their standing silhouettes
Behind the makeshift tables, the stretched sheets
Heaped high with sunglasses and brass-clasped leatherette –
And only disregard from the Sunday crowd, the slow mockery of feet.
How black they are. The night unpierced by stars
Absorbs less light than them, but they throw off passing stares
And make an emptiness of themselves, like the desperate anywhere.

Who on earth would want their desolate luxury?
The dark rows of sunglasses gazing at the sky
They stand listless guard over the daylight fakery
Without a word, a pleasantry – not even a welcome lie.
Come see, come touch. Instead they keep watch
Their genius is this: to haul away their catch
And be bodily transformed to nothing, whilst we see nothing much.

A police car, still far away, and the drivers in sunglasses
The very same as these, but wearing the authority of a brow,
Swims slowly downstream and makes several passes
Each time the men draw further into their own halo
Seeming trees, railings, dark ghosts with bundles and table-cases.
It passes. They are men again, and upon all their faces
Their feelings. One works his mouth in fear and dumbly paces

But another looks down the road in bold indifference
And unties his bundle so it flashes out like a cry
And hears his mother's sharp voice: have some sense
A childish act like that – you'll lose your living, boy
The police car begins again its fateful round
At last he bends to gather plastic from the ground
And bears it on his shoulder like a wound.

Now he slips into the crowd, for the crowd is sweet
Unfettered, desiring pleasure, bearing its own cheap goods
Constant, like the tide, it swells to fill the street
And those borne in it have no past and no roots:
They have forgotten the enterprise of migration
And believe again in the hibernation
Of swallows in the water's deep.

Sweet Companions

After Marina Tsvetaeva

On the next day there was a funeral for the traveller boy.
All the travellers came and stopped for the day
And formed a procession, for he had been a golden one
Cut down in flight by a car without headlights on.
Two twin girls walked behind the coffin
Keening like lost hens, arm in arm and sobbing
They were peaches, thought the men, ripe for the picking.
Pick us, they urged silently, our mouths are old with sobbing
So place your hands on us and be our first intimation of
Death. And these men, whose core was empty as an oak
Pared from them by wasp and rot and the sight of him
Laid out like a splintered choir boy, needed no second
Asking. Telling that night the tall tales of bravery
About the fire, not on the steppe as the fiery sun
Is eaten by the earth, but alongside the dump
Where the vans are parked up, in a stink of green
And shit, and two signs say no pikeys we say no paying
For pikeys there is no humility nor yet cast asunder
Nor yet touched by death and I tell you like an evangelist
There are places where love is still possible tangled in lust
Like two bodies, and sons born of the earth's dust
Which ate the sun as it dipped
Behind the municipal recycling and resource renewal plant
Which passes round here by the name of tip.

Laughter

When I awoke it had snowed
And it was the old geological snow
Snow upon snow, snow
Upon snow, and the sky was wet clay
As if the potter's wheel had just ceased spinning
When I awoke, the farmer pushed back the steel door
Of the barn, and the cows were blinded.

Not a week before when the hose to the trough
Split out there on the down, the water sprinkled out
Like manna from heaven, and settled on every blade
A million glass thumbs all pointing upwards:
Spare him, that even with his wound
He made a ring of beauty.

We went over the fields
And the mist met the snow, which had found every berry
Wised itself to the holly curl,
The fox had gone, but he had danced a new time –
And into the woods bent down like wild beasts to veer
Fast over ditches and warm streams licking brown leaves
To themselves, fast like that, there was a sound coming from us
And it was laughter.

Wolstonbury

for my children

I leave to my children Wolstonbury Hill
An island in the morning, with the mist at its heel
Pressing like a tide at its silent green slopes –
Day at the top – yet the underworld sleeps.

In winter the dewpond slithers with ice
And the trough glances back with the swiftness of skies
The branches are empty that the moth-wren shook
Where we broke our path through the wreck of the dock.

I saw a crow and her damp children once
They squatted and watched the cows from a fence
The calves trailed bloody umbilical cords
I never thought crows to be tender before –

Wind-kicked, the hawthorn's a stumbling boy –
But a blossoming hawthorn once witnessed joy
I have not breathed enough of the steep of the hill
But none of our kind ever quite had their fill.

In summer we climb the steps of thin root
And hear the grass squeal and wrench underfoot
And the blood in our ears and the scratch from the briar:
Are all the proof we need we're alive.

Yarrow and ragwort, clover and thyme
The earth echoes hollow. It says: I am your home.
And you have lain down so often to touch
The bedstraw, the sheep's bit, the violet, the vetch.

This is your hill and this is your home
I bequeath it to you, and here you will come
And here you shall be kings and walk tall –
And be crowned by the buzzard, like Wolstonbury Hill.

(I do not think there's a luckier king
Than he that knows how the skylarks sing –
Like unravelling tangles of sky-blue wool
And that I learnt on Wolstonbury Hill.)

Wolstonbury Hill – a finger of sound
A knuckle, a kneecap, a grassed shoulder-round
Take care of my children, and let them be still
On the bright palm of Wolstonbury Hill.

Late winter, like the tide retreating,
Throws ever hollower frosts across the grass
A complicated battle has been won, a port taken
The ships of spring allowed to pass
Still under the dead of night, and crasser
Greasier, shrunk – inconceivable like frozen rope
And still for many days it is unclear:
Winter cycles jaunty out to see his lover
A rifle slung across his shoulder
And ambushed, cannot even muster fear.
How can fortunes change this fast?
Light is suddenly divided and increased
Like a flank action stemming in the south
Shivering with redwings in the hedge
Faltering with spring's irresolute core.
Is this the meaning then of war?
A few hours when all hangs in the balance
And spring prepares to hang its head in shame
And who knows why winter then surrenders?
How every trembling victory is the same –
And history, happening like the seasons,
Spring is righteousness upon despair
And with a thousand pretty reasons
Trusses winter, beats it, shaves its hair.

Blessing

for Livvy and Jamie

That your love may be a walled garden
Newly tattered by rain, which comes suddenly
And stutters its few pearls on the lady's mantle

And in this walled garden, which is your love
Lupins spread their fingers, honeysuckling
Moths bear the walls' patterns, goldfinches tap –

Teasels tickle. This for you, who are no ordinary lovers
Who drink rain and mist and above all light
That dances and creeps and hopes

That your love may be wild and rampant
Multiplying like the mysterious foxgloves
Sweet and persistent as mallow

Fire-tipped like phlox
In its fierce dance of reconciliation
And meadowsweet and woodruff

Come to scent the cool halls of your
Marriage. Your love is a walled garden
May season follow season

Scent follow scent
The pattern of love flourish and root itself
Deeper and wider and lay its own seeds

Bluebell and harebell and comfrey and sage:
In the naming of love how sweet it grows
A hundred greening names to your young garden

In its ancient walls. Your love
Is a walled garden, and yet there will be
No name to contain it